Romance

Oliver Forward

Romance
Copyright © 2024 by Oliver Forward

ISBN: 979-8895310274 (hc)
ISBN: 979-8895310250 (sc)
ISBN: 979-8895310281 (e)

All rights reserved. No part of this publication may be reproduced, distributed, or transmitted in any form or by any means, including photocopying, recording, or other electronic or mechanical methods, without the prior written permission of the publisher and/or the author, except in the case of brief quotations embodied in critical reviews and other noncommercial uses permitted by copyright law.

The views expressed in this book are solely those of the author and do not necessarily reflect the views of the publisher, and the publisher hereby disclaims any responsibility for them.

Writers' Branding
(877) 608-6550
www.writersbranding.com
media@writersbranding.com

Contents

An Empty Dream 1

The Artist Portrait Of A Beautiful Woman 2

My Darling, I Feel This Way 4

I Was Born To Be Loved If Not 6

I'm Bound Forever 8

My Mind Overflows Like A River 9

Sometimes I Cry 10

The First Time We Kissed 11

The Password Is Love 12

This World Seems So Empty Without You 13

When You Embrace Me 15

Wrap Me 16

You Are My Thoughts 17

You're The One 18

After All These Years 20

An Empty Dream

Written by Oliver Forward
Music by Joshua David Walker

Oh my love, oh my love
Without you my life has become and empty dream
There is nowhere for me to run
I've been made drunk over your charm
Your love has left me in a storm
No one has heard my scream
Oh my love, oh my love
Without you my life has become and empty dream
Everything seems to look the same
I ask myself why should I live my life in vain
Believe me my heart has been pumping like a runaway train
Thoughts are going through my head like a movie scene
Oh my love, oh my love
Without you my life has become an empty dream
Tell me, what am I to do
Deep down inside of me I want this thing to change
What I'm feeling is so strange
These tears of mine are falling like rain
I need to be redeemed from the pain
Oh my love, oh my love
Without you my life has become an empty dream
Not having you by my side is driving me insane
At my age I refuse to play childish games
I do not want anyone to make the wrong claim
Hoping you'll understand what I mean
Oh my love, oh my love
Without you my life has become an empty dream

The Artist Portrait Of A Beautiful Woman

Written by Oliver Forward
Music by Joshua David Walker

When an artist makes preparation to paint a portrait
Only to describe a woman's beauty
He mixes all the colors together before the artist submerges
the tip of the brush into the paint
God takes his finger and places it into the center of the paint and injects melanin into the paint
The artist dips the tip of the brush back into the paint
A miracle takes place
The true essence of beauty is born
As the beauty gravitates to the picture frame and there
the woman's beauty makes it's claim
The artists brush leaves a deep refined line
To identify the texture of the woman's skin
The artists unlocks the imagination of his gifted mind
And begins to paint her long silky eyelashes
Hanging like angel wings as they glide through the wind
The woman's distinctive eyebrows shine like the rays of the sun
The artist soaks in the bathtub of his emotions
as the paint brush bristles opposed to the varied
of colors of the irresistible lips
Penetrating from the artistic mind of the artist he paints a picture of a beautiful body
The artist, being so amazed by his painting,

steps back to look at the painting
And walks away and decides to call
this portrait his masterpiece
The artist starts crying because he could not paint a
portrait of her inner heart
Her personality, her intellect, her radiance, her wittiness,
her kindness
But most of all how beautiful she was on the inside
All the artist could do was to place his face in his hands
Fall on his knees and cry
The artist portrait of a beautiful woman

My Darling, I Feel This Way

Written by Oliver Forward
Music by Joshua David Walker

My darling
I just feel this way
I realized that my pain for you has become
the metal shackles to my empty heart
I can never surrender to the idea of not being
loved by you This is my life
I promise not to liberate myself from the controlling
beast on the inside of me called love
I often cry the world's greatest sea
Which is made from my own salted tears
Without you, I'm in trouble
I feel so broken inside at times
Feeling inadequate, lonely and doubtfulness has set in
My emotions seem to outweigh the reality of life
I understand one can not achieve
all the desires of an over flowing heart
Therefore I often find myself just thinking about love
I want to talk love
I want to hear love
I want to see love
I want to smell love
I want to taste love
I want to eat love
I want to drink love

I want to walk with love
I want to touch love
I want to hold love
I want to squeeze love
I want to kiss love
I want to make love
I want to feel love
I'll just die in love
I'm just a slave for your love
I want you to unlock the imagination of my thirsty heart
Take the keys of pain and set me free
Let my love drain, drain, drain into your moist sea
If not, until then I must confess I am so in love with you
I just feel this way
Will you marry me my darling?

I Was Born To Be Loved If Not

Written by Oliver Forward
Music by Joshua David Walker

I was born to be loved
If not, I would be like a fish trying to swim without water
I was born to be loved
If not, I would like someone having a crush with no one to love
I was born to be loved
If not, I would be the only man in this world with no one to confess my love to
I was born to be loved
If not, I would be like a love song with no one to sing to
I was born to be loved
If not, I would be like a disfigured face but having not a smile
I was born to be loved
If not, I would be like a person having a huge empty hole in his heart with no one to fill it
I was born to be loved
If not, I would live my life as the lonely lover at the end of life living with a broken heart
I was born to be loved
If not, I would be like the moon, not able to give light to a darkened world by night
I was born to be loved
If not, I would be like someone falling in love with me but I can't love them back

I was born to be loved

If not, I would be like a dried up rose all the substance is there but the fragrance is gone

I was born to be loved

If not, I would be like being in love but having no one to love me back

I was born to be loved

If not, I would be like a blade of green grass trying to survive in the middle of the desert without water

Knowing the chances are very slim

I was born to be loved

If not

I'm Bound Forever

Written by Oliver Forward
Music by Joshua David Walker

I'm bound forever

I'm lying here talking to my soul

There is so much pressure on me that my heart has sprung a serious leak

This may not matter to you

That all my love is running out of me

This has been going for a long time

I keep laughing to myself

It is so amazing how you have captured my mind

The stars have consumed my eyes

I often feel your deep slow breathing constructing the walls of my soul

I want you to pull my love into your heart so you will be spell bound to me forever

As the water from the waves of the sea my love has become a broken compass

Just the thought of you intrigues me

I'm lying here talking to my mind

I'm bound forever

My Mind Overflows Like A River

Written by Oliver Forward
Music by Joshua David Walker

My mind overflows like a river
When I think of you I long for your precious arms to embrace me
All of my dreams are filled with soft gentle kisses
The precious memories you and I had together
I will always cherish the times you touched me with love in your hands
As the winds sings behind the background of the misty blue sky
Leaving a sparkle in my eye
To hear your enormous heart beating next to mine
I had no choice but to admire you, cherish, honor and respect you
Because you were so kind
When I die always remember that your love was buried
with me next to my soul
I can never forget the harmony of my thoughts that are sealed
beneath the components of my imagination
There is a cloud of love pouring upon my face that can never be replaced
I will always see you in my thoughts
Oh my love, your kindness is so deep inside of me
Reminds me of the roots of a palm tree planted by the edge of the sea
In the meantime I'll just keep lying here on the ocean shore of my
mind And daydream in and out of time
My mind overflows like a river

Sometimes I Cry

Written by Oliver Forward
Music by Joshua David Walker

Sometimes I cry because I'm sad
Sometimes I cry because of things I never had
Sometimes I cry when I think about my past
Sometimes I cry because my love doesn't last
Sometimes I cry because true love is hard to find
Sometimes I cry because my brother and sisters minds are locked back in time
Sometimes I cry because the fathers are not in their homes therefore their families live alone
Sometimes I cry because a system that is not for me but only in my mind I'm free
Sometimes I cry because we've lost sense of right and wrong
Sometimes I cry because we have lost our morals
Sometimes I cry because people are homeless
Sometimes I cry because we do not tell the truth when we teach the bible
Sometimes I cry because we have been taught self hate
Sometimes I cry because we don't just love each other like we should
Sometimes I cry because

The First Time We Kissed

Written by Oliver Forward
Music by Joshua David Walker

The first time we kissed it was like falling in love with time
My mind was scattered like wild grapes on a vine
I shook like a leaf on a tree waiting for the wind to use it's brakes
Oh that beautiful face of yours reminds me of a full moon at midnight
Coming out for fresh air
Your smile was bright and your eyes gave light that replaced the sun
The thick comet grey clouds attached to the blue
Being overtaken by the birds singing love songs that were true
I asked myself were you from outerspace
Every moment with you was time well spent
Yes, when you kissed me love opened the door of my heart
Now you're controlling my life like a strong surging wave of the sea
I'm going to love you and tell you that I love you
Until you believe me because
I just can't forget the first time we kissed

The Password Is Love

Written by Oliver Forward
Music by Joshua David Walker

The password is love
People have forgotten the password to life
The password is love
The world seems to have become drunken with selfishness
The password is love
No one seems to believe anyone could touch their life
The password is love
Our conversations have been ambushed by cell phones and texting
No one talks anymore
The password is love
Relationships have become like doctor Thomas F. Freeman's debate team
Everyone wants first place
The password is love
People do not make plans anymore to fall in love
The password is love
People are falling in love with things not people
The password is love
What is the meaning of love
Keep loving behind hurt
The password is love
Love is a duty
The password is love

This World Seems So Empty Without You

Written by Oliver Forward
Music by Joshua David Walker

When you left, this world seems so empty without you
I've never experienced a love storm before now
I'm looking through the front door of my soul,
The wind chimes are blowing and singing opera from the eve of my mind
I imagine, that you and I can live in love above the glory of the clouds
Without you, there are times I feel so hopeless
I keep asking myself where did I go wrong
I'm trying to so hard to forgive you,
but I can't forgive myself for falling in love with you
Now, I don't know what to do
I have given away all my emotions along with my heart
Still I am left wanting you
All of you is locked inside of me
I just can't get you out of my mind
After all these years of loving you and the changes we have gone through
Believe me my darling I am still in love with you
There is this huge hole down in my soul
All my life is flowing out of me like a river
This world seems so empty without you
My love was true, no one on earth can ever love you, the way I do, never ever

I love you so much, not to have you
I'd rather live my life trying to adjust to this silent pain
My skin has wrinkled like a garment
because through life I have given too much of myself away each day, I'm dying slowly
Wherever I go in life there is this wet trail of tears I leave behind
Only if you could follow the tear tracks maybe you'd find your way back into my heart
I've cried for so long that I almost drowned because
I never learned how to swim in my own tears
I'm waiting for your life jacket of love to save me
I'm tired of tasting my own salty tears
I will never stop loving you
I wanted you so bad last night
This world seems so empty without you

When You Embrace Me

Written by Oliver Forward
Music by Joshua David Walker

When you embrace me with your love
There's a strong desire that scorches the walls of my soul
I have become a passenger riding on your everlasting wings of love
Oh how I wish that I could be a part of the vessel that carries your love to certain parts of your body
I want to lay against the walls of your emotions and sleep the night away Only if I had the power to control night and day
I would find a way to stay inside of you
I think about the times when you and I kiss
I can feel your love covering the inner part of my soul
To live in this world without you would be like the sun having light but refusing to shine
The soft touch of your hands inspires every part of me
Your eyes have the ability to motivate the light from the sun
Your soft smooth skin always giving birth to love
Your delicate ears record the voice of the wind
The magic of your completeness drives away all my struggles and pain
When you embrace me

Wrap Me

Written by Oliver Forward
Music by Joshua David Walker

Oh my darling, would you wrap me in the cavity of your love?
Just the joy of waiting to be buried in the paradise of your sacred heart of love
Your personality has walked up and down the emotions of my soul
What I'm about to tell you is true
The rhythm of my heart refuses to beat the same
There is no one else to blame
Your love has been deeply engraved into my brain
I often gaze into the moon light only to call out your name
My love for you is so hot that it gives the sun its name
Must I face this world on my own?
Knowing that my struggle is greater than my pain
This forceful love is deeper than a bucket that travels through the well of my soul
Only if I could draw love from the vault of your mind
Oh my darling, would you wrap me in the cavity of your love

You Are My Thoughts

Written by Oliver Forward
Music by Joshua David Walker

You are my thoughts
My emotions have been torn like unwanted paper
My tears have grown legs and run straight down my face
Each day falling lower and lower
I'm feeling out of place
I think life sometimes seems unfair at the moment
I'm the only one who seems to care
It is so hard for me to say goodbye
Wondering at times should I break down and cry
I have found serenity in the rocking chair of my soul
Everything I know about you is locked behind the memories of time
Now, I'm lying here walking through the canal of my mind
Only if I could build a stairway back to the center of your soul
Because this love I have for you has gotten out of control
I just can't stop myself from loving you
My love is just too strong
Your face is posted on the theater walls of my dreams
I can hear the soft, sweet tone of your voice speaking as if there were a small mic pinned under my skin
Your voice seems to speak through the hunger
I smell your scent moving with the pillow of the clouds
I feel your hands caressing mine
I close my eyes as I lay inside the bedroom of my heart
Looking at the ceiling of my imagination knowing
I will always be in love with you
Because you are my thoughts

You're The One

Written by Oliver Forward
Music by Joshua David Walker

You're the one my love, you give me so much security
Knowing that I have you, there are no complaints
You support all my dreams as if they were your own
You are inspiring to me whether it be physically or mentally it does not matter
You are sweeter than natural honey and more valuable than money
You are the answer to all my fairy tales
I'm so eager now to hear the wedding bells, You are so elegant
I can't overlook the most classic wedding dress of all time
Your smile, is like the fringes on the wedding dress, that blow in the wings of the air
Oh my love, your love is as tender as a soft warm blanket
Only to give comfort to a new born baby, as it enters unfamiliar air
You are the one, because you're so special
That the giant of a man would feel safe
He would feel comfortable sharing his emotions, as you cradle him in your motherly arms
He will build you a home and not just a house,
but a home is where you belong
He will plant in your womb a seed of life, giving you beautiful children
Because you have become his darling wife
Understanding that there will be some cold days and dark nights
But both of us will always choose the things that are right
I must be the happiest man in all the world

Oh my darling, you are my hot and sexy girl
Oh my love you always sing my praise song
As if I was the only man to rule this land
My sweetheart you are so wonderful and easy to talk to
You are so considerate, compassionate and empathic
The meanest person in the world would love to be your friend
You my love are the best,
You're loyal as the yellow on gold
You're like heaven's home to the soul
You're the one, You're the one

After All These Years

This saga takes place in the year of 1978. Salathiel, by name, found himself one dewy morning as he boarded the city bus. Walking eight to ten seats from the front of the bus, he noticed the dissension in the atmosphere. The misery that is always associated with the lack of companionship came to an end when the air shocks of the bus caught the metal of the wheels with a loud whistle. Salathiel could not control his big brown eyes. For the first time, Salathiel's dream had come true. There stood a tall, beautiful paper sack brown skinned lady. Her legs were bowed like a bow and arrow. As she stepped onto the bus, the scent of her perfume penetrated through the wind and into his nose. Her high cheekbone complimented her long silky eyelashes. Her mouth was full, and her lips were like a honeycomb chisel with the perfect radius in shape for the right color of lipstick. The dimples in her cheeks were deep as a valley inside her skin. Right away Salathiel knew that it was love at first sight. However, each step she made in his direction, the weaker he became and the stronger his desire for her grew. Slowly she found her way to a seat in front of him. Her hair was black as midnight, so thick perhaps; if one would touch it, he would become lost. Salathiel's mouth was locked in silence. He noticed two other men staring at her lavish beauty. Salathiel could not think clearly because of the stain love made on his heart. The day went by so slowly, and all that night he tossed and turned hoping that it would skip away. Salathiel could not wait to look into her light, glossy eyes again.

The next day, Salathiel arose early and dressed quickly as possible. And this time, he passed up the bus stop and walked to hers, which was about two miles away. As he approached the bus stop, no one was there. Salathiel stood and waited. Finally, she arrived looking as beautiful as a sun shiny day. "Good morning," said Salathiel, She replied- searching for words to say. Salathiel was afraid that he would say the wrong thing.

His conversation became anxious. He asked questions like, "Do you live in this section of town?" Rebecca replied, "Well, my step-father lives here." Salathiel didn't quite understand her family's living arrangement, but he was well pleased to be holding a conversation with her. He stared into her cherry- colored mouth with every expression she made. He was desperately craving to kiss the moistness that separated her lips. He felt the desire deep within his soul. And before one could realize how fast time was getting away, that loud noise was again reborn from the wheels of the bus that brought it to a halt. And Rebecca would say, "Goodbye. I'll see you tomorrow." Salathiel walked away with a smile.

From then on, every day seemed as if it was the first day they met. Salathiel concluded that he must tell her he loved her with no end, but he could not because he'd only known her for a short time. One day, when the bus reached Rebecca's pickup stop, she was not there. Salathiel's world became unbelievably empty. There were not enough hours in the day to express the absence of her. Weeks and months passed; however, she was nowhere to be found. For now, loneliness was back into his life again, Salathiel stated to himself. Each day as the bus made its routes, whenever it would approach Rebecca's stop, and she wasn't there. It seemed as if a part of Salathiel's life was stolen away. One Monday after heavy storms, the air shocks caught the metal of the wheels again. Salathiel looked down. It was uniquely Rebecca as she stepped on the bus. This time she was not by herself. Her perfectly round and protruding stomach beat the rest of her through the door of the bus. Salathiel's heart panicked. He felt as if he were going to throw up. "How could she do something like that," he said to himself. His heart was broken for the first time. The deception of love was on target, hitting his heart at an extreme time of his youth. There was no defense. His heart fell hard through his stomach, down to his legs, wrapped around his ankles, and shattered on the ground. He became so empty all day. The dark nights. Unfortunately, there was no longer any confidence nor excitement in walking to the bus, only an empty view without a picture frame.

Months later, Rebecca again stepped on the bus. It seemed she would have the baby as soon as she sat. Salathiel could not stop looking at her, how the change in her brought about a glow. It seemed as if God put the sun in her face, drawing the love from Salathiel even through the hurt. Salathiel said within himself, "I don't care if she is pregnant by some other man, his love can't be stronger than mine. I love her with no end! My love takes over the claim!" Aggressive time took her away, not from his heart. Salathiel could not forget her. Every time the bus would pass by her stop minutes away from her stepfather's house, he tried to put the dream behind, but true love prevailed. As he looked through the air, Rebecca's seat was empty. Often times, Salathiel would sit there as if she would come and sit next to him.

One day, Salathiel's hunger for love drove him to the front door of her stepfather's house. Salathiel knocked repeatedly. Suddenly the door is opened, and a tall older and seasoned man greets Salathiel. "Hello, sir", Salathiel replied. "May I help you, young fellow?" "My name is Salathiel, and I'm I here to check on Rebecca." The older man responded, "Oh thank you, young man, but I'm sorry, she moved a few months ago about ten miles from here to a community called Glen Burnie." Salathiel knew that his chances of seeing her again looked mighty slim. Salathiel didn't own a car, so he worked hard to save for a down payment. Eventually, he purchased a 1979 Chevy hatchback, just enough room for Rebecca and the baby. Off to Glen Burnie he went not knowing the street or the address, but just the idea that he was closer to her gave him all the joy that any man could have. Up and down the streets he drove, desperately, as if he was searching for his own life. Months passed as he repeated this routine on a daily basis. Finally, he gave up, for the love trail of Rebecca could not be traced. The area was too large and diverse in population. For sure he had lost her again, and maybe forever. Day in and day out, he thought of her. Often times, he would drive through the neighborhood, refusing to discontinue his useless search. Sixteen years to be exact, Salathiel was attending a funeral service and a light intercepted his eyes. Rebeccas was waving through a crowd. Salathiel was suddenly overwhelmed and felt that rush which he had felt during his initial meeting. The advancement that was made was broken because of the crowd and due to the massive crowd, again they were divided from one another. Salathiel experienced hurt that could not be avoided. Distasteful knowledge taught him that love was the most powerful feeling on earth.

Salathiel's life maturely changed after some twenty years. One sunny Thursday, as he was looking at some apartments, he knocked on this particular door. Standing behind it was Rebecca. Speechless, Salathiel looked into her marquis framed glossy dove-like eyes with amazement. Unfortunately, Mother Nature had made a few adjustments. Standing beside her, clinging to her waist was a little boy holding onto love. Another lad, almost Salathiel's height was leaning against her shoulder with a smile. For the first time, the lad not knowing the father he never had, and Salathiel saw the son he never knew. The endearment for Rebecca's beauty was still there as it was in the fall of 1978. That he still loved her was evident, after all these years.

www.ingramcontent.com/pod-product-compliance
Lightning Source LLC
LaVergne TN
LVHW041603070526
838199LV00047B/2118